# ALL-AGE
## LeNT · eaSTeR

# ALL-AGE
# LENT · EASTER

## Ideas, talks and games for services

**NICK HARDING**

**kevin mayhew**

First published in 2002 by
KEVIN MAYHEW LTD
Buxhall, Stowmarket, Suffolk IP14 3BW
Email: info@kevinmayhewltd.com

9 8 7 6 5 4 3 2 1 0

ISBN  1 84003 990 6
Catalogue No.  1500551

Cover design by Angela Selfe
Edited by Elisabeth Bates
Typeset by Louise Selfe

Printed and bound in Great Britain.

# Contents

# About the author

Nick Harding grew up in Birmingham, where he learned about Christianity from an early age. After going through the education system he taught in Nottinghamshire and has worked with a number of Christian organisations in a variety of roles ever since. Nick writes articles for a range of magazines and has written many books for and about working with children. He works as Children's Mission Support Officer for Southwell Diocese, supporting rural and urban churches in their work. Nick is a fan of the music of Elton John and Elgar, enjoys working out at the gym and walking in Sherwood Forest, and shares his life with his wife Clare, and sons Jared and Callum.

# Introduction

The period before Easter is often a hard time. It is before the new shoots of spring are really showing themselves, and before the weather has improved from the darkness of winter. In the Church it is a time to remember Jesus' suffering and challenge in the desert wilderness, and a time when many believe we should 'go without' something that we enjoy.

Even if you manage to survive the Lent season, Easter looms, and again it is all too often seen as a time of sadness and darkness. True, Jesus had to suffer and die, but we must remember that he rose again, bringing eternal light to darkness.

Lent is a good time to reflect, have a spiritual 'clean up', and be aware of all that Jesus went through for us. This should lead us on to Easter, when we vividly recall Jesus' pain, and actively celebrate his life.

This book contains many suggestions to help all-age Lent and Easter services and activities. There are games to do with some or all of the congregation, prayers to learn, repeat or use from the front, opening prayers and sentences in accessible language, and activities for family groups and others to do during a service. There are also talk suggestions and outlines. There is enough here to keep your church going for many Lent and Easter seasons in the future.

# Activities and games

This range of activities and games is designed to be used with the congregation, and many encourage the congregation to get into groups or pairs. Some require prepared items and equipment, which are always listed at the beginning of each suggestion.

## The cost of confession

*You will need: pens and paper for all the congregation.*

Ask everyone to write down three things they have done wrong over the past few days. Remind adults that they may need to help children with the writing. Then ask a willing volunteer, possibly 'primed' before you begin, to read out their list. Ask the congregation to award the price of each confession, on a scale of '1' – not very serious, to '5' – very serious indeed. After some suggestions remind everyone that we have all sinned, and God forgives us however serious our wrongs may be, and Jesus made that forgiveness possible. Ask the congregation to keep the pieces of paper 'confessions' for a prayer activity later, and finish the activity by reminding the congregation that confession must be part of our thanks to Jesus.

## Shrove and Ash

*You will need: pens, paper.*

Briefly explain the meanings and purpose of Shrove Tuesday and Ash Wednesday.

Shrove Tuesday was the day when people cleared out their larders and food stores, eating pancakes to use everything up. This marked the beginning of a period of reflection and confession in memory of

Jesus in the wilderness. The word 'Shrove' is derived from the medieval word 'shrive', which means to confess our sins and be forgiven.

Ash Wednesday is the first day of the confession and reflection period. When people confessed all that they had done wrong to God they used to dress in hard, rough sackcloth and mark themselves in black ash from their fires as a sign that they were sorry.

Ask the congregation to form small groups of families and others, and write an acrostic poem or series of sentences to explain Shrove Tuesday and Ash Wednesday, based on the words SHROVE and ASH. An example would be:

Saying sorry
Hearing God speak
Removing all temptation
Only thinking about God
Very important
Everyone should do it
Asking for forgiveness
Serious about God
Hoping to be better

## Peculiar pancakes

*You will need: a range of sweet and savoury foods (e.g. onion, honey, lemon, ham, jam, cheese, etc.), four ready-cooked pancakes, two blindfolds.*

No Lent is complete without pancakes! Explain the origin of pancakes – to use up the rich food and prepare for a period of restraint. Then ask for two parent-and-child pairs to come to the front. Blindfold the adults, and ask the children to choose two of the foods available to put into a pancake for their parent to eat! Fill two pancakes with the chosen ingredients and ask the adults to eat them. Then if there is time repeat the process with another two couples.

## Tempting times

*You will need: sheets of A3 or flipchart paper, marker pens.*

Ask the congregation to get into large family groups, remembering to remind them to invite others to join them, especially people in church alone. Give each group a sheet of paper and a marker pen and ask them to each write on the sheet things they find tempting. You may want to give them a few things to begin their thinking from your own experience. Examples could be eating too much chocolate, wanting things that belong to others, or always wanting to be in charge.

## Giving it away

As a church you could plan in advance to have a particular charity, cause or fundraising effort during the 40 days of Lent. Then encourage all of the congregation, whatever their age, to give something up that may cost money, and give that saved money to the fund. This not only helps focus the mind on the charity or cause in hand, but also challenges the congregation to take Lent seriously. You could do this in conjunction with 'Giving it up'.

## Speed eating

*You will need: a bag with four pairs of items of food in it such as two apples, two lumps of cheese, two raw carrots, two cold burgers, two yoghurt drinks, two biscuits, etc.*

Invite two people from the congregation to come to the front. Explain that Shrove Tuesday was a day to quickly eat up all the food before the 40 days of Lent, and this is a chance for speed-eating too! Then the volunteers should race each other, eating one pair of food items at a time. If you have time repeat it with the second pair of food items, and so on.

## Giving it up

*You will need: OHP and pens or flipchart.*

Remind the congregation that Lent is often a time when people take the opportunity to give things up. Sometimes people give up things like chocolate or other things which they don't need. Lent is not necessarily a time for us to punish ourselves, but giving up some luxury for the season does us no harm, and reminds us all of what Jesus gave up when he went to the desert for 40 days.

Ask members of the congregation to shout out something they will give up for the Lent period, making sure that you have a mix of adults and children making the suggestions. Write up the suggestions so that everyone can see the range of suggestions. It may then be appropriate to move in to a time of quiet and prayer.

## Finding space

*You will need: a tape or CD of quiet, tranquil music.*

Ask everyone in the congregation to stand and move around until they have found somewhere quiet and away from other people. Parents may want to take young children with them. Then play the quiet music, asking everyone to imagine what it must have been like for Jesus to go alone into the wilderness for so long.

After a short time slowly and clearly read out the account of Jesus in the wilderness from Luke 4:1-13. Allow a little more quiet with the music playing before reading out the next verse (14). Then invite the people to return to their seats.

## What everyone wants

Ask all of the congregation to stand and silently think of one thing that they would really like to have or be. They may want to have a big house, a new car, or to be a pop star or sports hero!

Then ask them to move around to people they do not know well, and share with each other their desires.

Finish by reminding them that Jesus was tempted with things the devil thought he desired, but Jesus' desire to do what was right was stronger.

## All that is important – Lent

*You will need: OHP, pens.*

Talk to the worshippers about all that Jesus gave up, stood against, and suffered in the wilderness. Remind them that he could have had everything he wanted, and all the power of the world was available to him if he had done what the devil suggested. But instead he was strong enough to resist the temptations that were put before him. Jesus considered that all the things that are important to the world were not important for him.

Write some of the following words on acetate and display them using an OHP. Encourage the congregation to watch as slowly you cross out each word.

Pride  Power  Self  Strength  Life  Comfort  Love  Authority

## Tempting times

*You will need: a set of cards with 1 to 5 on them, chocolate bars.*

Ask for three children to volunteer. Explain that they are in a race from the back of the church to the front, and they can step forward the number of steps that they pick from the cards. At the end there is not a prize, just the satisfaction of knowing that they have got there!

Begin the race, holding the cards down and shuffling them so that they do not know which number they pick each time. From time to time tempt the racers, particularly the one at the back, with a chocolate bar if they drop out of the race, trying to be as persuasive as possible! Continue the race until one child is the winner, and share all remaining bars of chocolate between those still in the race. Finish by reminding the congregation that Jesus was tempted with much more than a chocolate bar, and he was strong enough to resist it.

## Good and bad

Ask the members of the congregation to stand and be ready to move around. Point out that one direction is where they go if the statement you make is good, and the opposite direction is where they should go if it is bad. Then read out some of these statements:

- Jesus went to be quiet in the wilderness.
- Jesus was tempted to turn a stone into bread.
- Jesus resisted the temptation.
- Jesus was challenged to worship the devil.
- Jesus said, 'The scripture says worship God alone.'

- The devil asked Jesus to prove his power by jumping off a cliff.
- Jesus did not jump.
- Jesus was left alone after the temptation.
- Jesus felt stronger, and had the power of the Holy Spirit with him.

## 40 days – part 1

*You will need: A4 paper, pencils.*

Introduce this activity before the service begins. Remind the congregation that Jesus spent 40 days in the wilderness, and in that time he was tempted. Then hand out some sheets of A4 paper and pencils, and ask for everyone to write on a sheet what they would like to do on a free day or a day off. Once that is done and most people have written down their ideal day collect in the sheets and pick up to five interesting-looking days to mention later, and then begin the service. This activity continues as '40 days – part 2'.

## 40 days – part 2

*You will need: A4 sheets used earlier, radio mic (if possible).*

Remind the congregation that earlier they wrote on the sheet what they would like to do on a free day. Then ask in turn for the people whose perfect days you have picked out as being interesting to tell everyone a little more about their day, moving around among the congregation with the radio mic to do so.

Finish by reminding the congregation that we have all got plenty of good ideas about what we would like to do for a day, but instead of doing something like that Jesus chose to spend 40 days without anything, living in a wild place and listening to God. Sometimes what we want to do is not the same thing as doing what would be best for us to do.

## Dice Easter

*You will need: 2 dice, OHP sheets of the six phrases below.*

Show the congregation the dice, and ask them to shout out the answers to the following questions:

- What is the lowest possible number from two dice? (2)
- What is the highest possible number from two dice? (12)

Then hold up one die. Ask the following questions:

- How many sides has it got? (6)
- What is the highest possible number? (6)
- What number can you get with one die that you can't get with two? (1)

Invite six people (a mix of ages) to come out, and give the first one the chance to shake one die and shout out the number. Then teach the congregation to say the phrase given below for the number they shook. Repeat this until all six numbers have been shaken, giving extra turns if a previous number is shaken again. You could keep the adults at the front while you tell the story (see Talks section).

    1 – One die was shaken

    2 – Two robbers on crosses

    3 – Three days later

    4 – Four nails

    5 – Five people at the tomb

    6 – Six o'clock in the evening

## Easter order

*You will need: the list of events below photocopied for groups in church to use, scissors, pens.*

Ask the congregation to split into mixed age groups, and then give each group a photocopied list and a pair of scissors. Ask one person in the group to cut out each of the events on the list, and the others to talk about the story of Easter while that is done. Then the group should put the events in order of their happening and number them in the correct order.

- Jesus started to carry his cross.
- Soldiers mocked Jesus.
- Jesus was arrested.
- A disciple tried to protect Jesus.
- At three Jesus cried out and died.
- Jesus claimed to be the Son of God.

- Jesus was beaten and spat at.
- Peter denied Jesus.
- Jesus was questioned by the Council.
- At noon it went dark.
- Pilate questioned Jesus.
- The crowd shouted, 'Crucify him.'
- Simon of Cyrene helped carry the cross.
- Jesus did not have the drink he was offered.
- Jesus was put on the cross at 9am.
- A sign was put over the cross.

## All that is important – Easter

*You will need: OHP and pens.*

Talk to everyone about the saving nature of the death of Jesus. He had to do it so that we could have a true relationship with God, and through his death we can be forgiven. Jesus died, and Jesus came alive again. In the same way we were dead as sinners, but we are alive and forgiven.

Write some of the following words on acetate and display them using an OHP. If you did the activity 'All that is important – Lent' it would be worth reminding the congregation that the words are the same, and Jesus again proved that the things that are important to the world meant nothing to him. Encourage the congregation to say each word slowly as you cross it out.

Pride   Power   Self   Strength   Life   Comfort   Love   Authority

## Jesus was

*You will need: cards with the numbers below written on them.*

Hand out the cards at random to families or small groups in the congregation.

23   26   29   32   34   36   37

Read out from Mark 15 and then ask each group to look up the verse on their card and work out what this has to say about Jesus. What was it about the way Jesus died that attracted the attention of the army officer? Then have one 'spokesperson' from each group come to the front to read their verse and explain what the group thought it tells us about Jesus.

## Lent lists/Easter lists

*You will need: paper and pens.*

Ask for two children to come out, bringing with them an adult each. Give the adult the paper and pen. Explain that you are going to say a word, and then in their pairs they must list as many other words as they can that are connected with the word you give them. After each round add up who has come up with the most words. Repeat the game with another word, and so on as time allows.

Lent words: Pancakes, Ash, Sorry, Forgiveness, Wilderness, Temptation

Easter words: Cross, Stone, Eggs, Crowd, Meal, Life

## The end of the journey

Explain that we all go on journeys. Some of our journeys are to do things, to see people, to get to school or home, or to do work. Then ask the congregation to think about and shout out what they would hope to find or do at the end of the following journeys. It may help if you can take a radio mic to them.

- A journey into the countryside.
- A journey on holiday.
- A journey to hospital to visit someone.
- A journey home after school.
- A journey to see a relative.
- A journey to a wedding or celebration.

Finish the activity by explaining that all through Jesus' life he knew that the end of the journey to Jerusalem would be the cross.

## The final meal

*You will need: Bible.*

Ask the congregation to close their eyes and picture Jesus and his disciples as they enjoyed the Passover meal together. Read the account of the Last Supper from Luke 22:14-22.

Then ask everyone to close their eyes as you say the following to describe the feelings that those present may have had:

- Jesus was sad, knowing that he would soon be arrested.
- Judas was guilty, knowing that he was going to cause Jesus pain.
- The disciples were confused – they still didn't fully understand.

## Arresting questions

*You will need: the following questions on sheets of paper, Blu-Tack.*

Before the service begins make sure that you have displayed the questions around the church in different locations. Read out Mark 14:43-50, and encourage the congregation to find the passage also. Then ask them to move around the church in twos or threes, reading the questions and discussing the possible answers. Allow plenty of time before asking everyone to sit back down and taking the questions down. If time allows read out each question, asking for comments as you do.

- What had Jesus being doing before the soldiers arrived?
- Why did Judas decide to betray Jesus?
- Do you think the guards and soldiers were really needed?
- Why was Jesus not arrested in the temple?
- Do you think Judas was a worse disciple than the others?

## Sad weekend

*You will need: the items listed below spread around the church, Easter hymns on CD or played by musicians.*

Place the items in different areas of the church, and ask the congregation to go in small groups or pairs from one item to another, look at them, and discuss quietly with each other what they have to do with the Easter story. At the same time have some Easter hymns playing quietly.

Items could include: a whip, thorns, nails, a cross, a cloth or bandage, a large stone, a bottle of perfume.

## Jesus is alive!

*You will need: mini Easter eggs, radio mic (if possible).*

Talk about Easter morning, and the excitement that some of the disciples must have experienced when they heard that Jesus was alive. Ask for people to think about other ways of expressing that Jesus is alive, by shouting a different phrase, dancing, waving arms, clapping, or whatever! Give each person who is brave enough to demonstrate to the congregation a mini egg.

## Thumbs up

Read out the following sentences, asking the congregation to give a 'thumbs up' to the good news part of each sentence, and a 'thumbs down' to the sad or bad news elements. If you can get hold of large foam thumbs (available at many cheap seaside shops!) they will add to the fun of the activity.

- Jesus shared a meal with his friends . . . and was arrested.
- Jesus was beaten and questioned . . . but remained calm.
- Peter denied knowing Jesus . . . but realised quickly that he had done wrong.
- Jesus carried his cross up the hill . . . and Simon of Cyrene helped.
- Jesus died on the cross . . . his last words were 'It is finished'.
- Jesus was taken from the cross . . . to a private tomb.
- Jesus' body was gone on the third day . . . he was alive!
- Mary could not find the body . . . but met Jesus instead.

# The King

*You will need: a supply of card, paper, glue, pens, scissors and pencils.*

Read out Luke 23:38, and explain that the sign was put on the cross above Jesus' head to make fun of him. Then ask the congregation to get into groups including all ages and any people on their own, and think of a sign they could make to describe Jesus. Then, using the card, paper and other resources, each group should make a sign to describe Jesus.

# Three times

*You will need: a stopwatch or watch with a seconds hand.*

Remind the worshippers of the account of Peter who was waiting in the courtyard and denied knowing Jesus three times. Then ask for four volunteers to come out and tell the story of Peter in the courtyard in turn. Each time one of the volunteers says the same word three times, and it can be any word, they are out of the game and the next person takes over until the story is completed. The winner is the one who talks for the most seconds before being out.

# Seen alive

*You will need: Bibles for all the congregation, the questions below on OHP sheet.*

Split the congregation into four, allocating a Gospel (Matthew, Mark, Luke, John) to each. They should then work in small family groups, exploring that Gospel to find out as much as they can about the appearances of Jesus after he came alive again. These questions could be up on OHP to help:

• How did Jesus appear?
• Who was it to?
• Did anyone touch Jesus?
• What did Jesus say?
• How did the people respond to seeing Jesus?
• What did the people do afterwards?

# Speaking out

*You will need: OHP and pens or flipchart.*

Read out the account of Jesus being crucified from Mark 15:21-32, and then pause for a few moments for everyone to picture the scene. Then read it again, asking them to imagine what the people there would have said. Then invite people to suggest what the following people may have been saying, writing up their suggestions on OHP or flipchart:

- Simon of Cyrene, who helped carry the cross.
- The guards and soldiers who nailed Jesus to the cross.
- The passers-by who were near.
- The 'religious' people.

# Talks

These talks follow a range of styles from letters and monologues to be read out with little explanation, to clear talks more based on a sermon style. Like most resources, they may not all be ideal for your situation, and therefore may require some adaptation.

## Feasting and fasting

*You will need: A CD, smart clothes, appetising food.*

Life can be a feast! We feast on living to the full, enjoying all that we have, and making the most of our possessions. We like to have the best, and most of us can simply go out and buy whatever we want whenever we want it.

*(Hold up CD)* We feast on the best (or some might say the worst) of music, and have really good sound quality from our CDs. We can listen to music, buy music, sing along to music, and read all about music. Life is a feast.

*(Hold up clothes)* We also like to wear nice things, even if, like stone-washed jeans, we want them to look old and used! We have fashions, change our clothes, and have plenty to choose from. Life is a feast.

*(Hold up the food)* Most of all we feast on food! We all like eating, and some of us like eating a little too much! We have so much to choose from, as any walk in a supermarket will show. There are all kinds of food available from all nations and for all tastes. Life is a feast, and we feast on the best.

Yet we all experience difficult times too, when we struggle to get through and feel that we have nothing and no hope. Only by experiencing the best do we have the hope we need in the hard times. The feast is good, but the times when we have not got all we want, or when things don't go our way, remind us just how good the good times are. Only by facing problems do we appreciate the good things that life offers.

Lent begins with the feast traditionally enjoyed on Shrove Tuesday, the name evolving from 'shrive', a medieval word meaning to confess and be forgiven. When we confess we say we are really sorry to God for all the things we do wrong. As we clear ourselves out at the beginning of Lent through confession, we do so in practical terms by using up food in pancakes. Then the Lent period, commemorating Jesus' time of fasting and temptation in the wilderness, includes a little fasting for us too.

Jesus spent 40 days without food so that he could win the battle against the devil, and so he could concentrate on his Father God. It would be daft for us to give up food, but we could give up something, so that we too could do good things and think about God.

## Jesus is tempted

*This is a straightforward retelling of the story of Jesus being tempted.*

It was going to be hard, and Jesus knew it. He set out to walk and live in the desert for over a month, and he had decided not to eat for all that time so he could think more about what he had to do, and talk more to his Father God.

As he walked, sat and slept in the heat of the desert Jesus became more and more hungry, until by the fortieth day he was very hungry indeed, and then it happened.

The devil sidled up to him and started to talk. 'You must be hungry,' he said. 'You must really like the thought of a piece of juicy bread.' Jesus listened as the devil continued, 'If you really are the Son of God, like you think you are, then why don't you turn those stones over there into bread? Go on, you can do it, and it would taste really good.' Jesus thought about it, and he would have really enjoyed eating some food, but he knew there were more important things in life. 'No,' said Jesus, 'the Bible says that God's words are more important than food.' The devil grunted and looked angry – he would have to find another way to trap Jesus.

After a while the devil said, 'Come on. We shall go to the top of that church over there,' and they did. Once there he said, 'Go on Jesus, throw yourself off. I'm sure angels would come along and help you if you're brave enough!' Jesus was not impressed. 'The Bible says not to put Father God to the test, so I won't!' said Jesus. The devil groaned and looked even more unpleasant.

A while later Jesus was standing on a high mountain admiring the view of many nations. The devil tried a third time: 'Hey, Jesus, if you bow down to me I'll give you all that to control. You will be in charge, honest!' Jesus was not tricked, and replied, 'Oh, go away! I will only worship God, not an evil character like you!' The devil was so cross that he went, leaving Jesus, the winner, on that desert hilltop.

## Pause for Thought

*This talk highlights some of the key points of the Lent season. During the talk there are times when you should encourage the congregation to stop and pause for thought, focused on the word given in bold. You may want to have these words displayed on OHP.*

Lent is traditionally a time to stop and think. In the busyness of our lives, with always lots to do at home, at school, at church, or at work, there is often not enough time to stop. So, during Lent, God invites us to slow down. Even now we may find it hard to sit really still, or to think about God. It is now time to pause for thought, and think about **stopping**.

Lent is a time when we can look at our own lives and decide what God may want to clear out. We sometimes spend our time doing things which we know are not right. We sometimes have anger inside us against someone or something. Now we can clear out the things that are wrong about ourselves, and ask God for forgiveness. It is now time to pause for thought, and think about **saying sorry**.

Lent is the time when we think about Jesus. We remember that he went from his home to live for many weeks in a wilderness. He was away from friends and family, without food and water. Jesus was willing to suffer like that because he knew it was the right thing to do. It is now time to pause for thought, and think about **Jesus suffering**.

Lent is the time when we remember that Jesus was tempted by the devil. The devil wanted Jesus to give his power over, and to worship evil. Jesus was hungry and tired, yet he remained strong and only did what he knew was right. He refused to give in to temptation. The power on offer was very attractive, but Jesus knew that God was stronger. It is now time to pause for thought, and think about **temptation**.

Lent is the time when we get ready for Easter. We remember that Jesus knew he was going to die, even though crowds cheered and waved palm leaves to welcome him into Jerusalem. We remember that Jesus suffered the pain of being tortured and whipped, and finally being hung on a cross with others watching and jeering. Lent helps us prepare to remember Jesus' pain, and celebrate that he came alive again. It is now time to pause for thought, and think about **Easter**.

# The road to Easter begins

*You will need: two very large signs placed at different points around the church, with the following on them: 'The Road' and 'The Temple'. For each section of this talk you will need to walk to the appropriate sign. It works much better if some or all of the congregation walk with you. This talk could be split into two sections, and used during different parts of the service.*

### Introduction

Did you know that many people who are in road accidents say that they experienced a strange sensation of powerlessness, as if everything is in slow-motion but there is nothing that they can do about it? They just have to brace themselves for the painful impact, and wait to see what damage is done.

In many ways the week before Easter, and events that took place, are the same. Jesus knew there was nothing to be done, as he had made his decision to do as the Father wanted, and he knew what pain he would face. His journey to Easter was painful, unavoidable, and unstoppable.

### Part 1 – The Journey to Jerusalem

The two disciples did what Jesus had told them. They had gone to a nearby village and found a colt tied up, and brought it for Jesus to ride. Then the crowds started to gather, cheering and shouting Jesus' name as he rode along the main road into Jerusalem, through the walls past the houses, and to the market place in the centre. As he rode, more and more joined those already gathered, and they all seemed happy. Yet Jesus knew that the end of the journey to Easter would be hard and painful for him.

### Part 2 – The Temple

Jesus went to the temple to pray and worship the Father God, but as he arrived he was shocked and saddened by what he saw. There were thieves and robbers there, people who sold things at high prices, and made lots of money illegally by cheating foreigners and visitors who changed money. As Jesus looked around and heard all the noise he shouted out, 'This should be God's house, but you have made it an evil place for robbers and cheats,' and with that he turned over the tables of the moneychangers. The religious leaders, who made a lot of money out of allowing the temple to be used as a market, watched what Jesus did and decided that Jesus must be stopped.

# 'J' for Judas

This talk looks at the life and activities of Judas before and during Easter. Ask the congregation to listen out for any words beginning with J and make a J-shape in the air every time they hear a J-word being said.

Jesus had chosen 12 disciples to be with him. They were not perfect people, but Jesus chose those whom he trusted and thought would be able to do the job of helping him. One of them was the energetic Judas Iscariot, a politician who wanted to change the world and get the Romans out of Galilee and the surrounding areas.

Judas went with Jesus as they travelled around Judea. Judas heard Jesus speak about healing, fairness and justice. He heard all the wise things that he said, and they saw Jesus do amazing miracles like making lame people walk and making blind men see, and saw the joy that Jesus shared. Judas also saw that the chief priests and religious leaders were getting jealous of the popularity that Jesus was gaining.

Judas listened carefully to all that Jesus said. He hoped that Jesus was really a king who would get an army of Jews together and fight the Romans so that the people could have their own land back. But as time went on he realised that Jesus was interested in bringing justice and peace rather than war, and he didn't understand. Soon he became angry. 'Why won't Jesus lead an army?' he thought to himself one day as he walked through the temple past a group of important Jewish priests. 'We need someone to lead us to Jesus and show us who he is, and we could pay them,' Judas overheard one of the Priests say, so he slowed down and listened more. The Priests didn't like Jesus and wanted to arrest him and put him in jail. Just at that moment Judas saw this as his chance to make a bit of money, so he said to the priests, 'I know where Jesus will be, and I'll take you to him tonight . . . but it will cost you thirty silver coins.' The priests handed over the money, and the deal was done.

As the disciples sat to eat with Jesus that evening Judas felt bad. Jesus was talking about how he would die, and about how one of the disciples would betray him, and in his heart Judas sensed that Jesus knew it would be him. After the meal Jesus and the disciples went to a garden to pray, and Judas led the soldiers and priests there to arrest Jesus.

The next day Judas felt sick and confused. He now understood that Jesus was more than just an army leader, he really was the Son of God. He tried to give the money back to the priests but they just laughed in his face and told him how Jesus was being sentenced to death with no justice and no jury. He tried to get to see Jesus but Jesus was in jail being beaten. So in the end Judas Iscariot spent the money on a field, where he hung himself a few days later, knowing that he had sent Jesus to his death.

Judas was like many of us. He knew that Jesus was special, but didn't realise just how special he was until it was too late. This Easter we can all discover Jesus for ourselves, and discover the joy that he can bring to our lives.

## The road to Easter ends

*You will need: two very large signs placed at different points around the church, with the following on them: 'The Garden' and 'The Cross'. As with 'The road to Easter begins' (above) it is much more effective if you and some or all of the congregation walk to the appropriate sign. This talk could be split into two sections, and used during different parts of the service.*

## Introduction

The journey that Jesus made was to his death. Jesus knew that he was going to die, and he also knew that his disciples didn't really understand what was going to happen. It is hard to imagine the pain and sadness that Jesus must have felt on these final journeys.

## Part 1 – The garden

Jesus took his disciples for a walk after their meal. He wanted some time and space to think and pray to God. He wanted to ask his Father to help him put up with all the pain that he knew was coming. As they walked up the rocky path Jesus told his disciples to keep a look out, to pray, and most of all to stay awake.

Jesus went on his own and sat down, crying out to God and telling him that he didn't really want to die. After a while has was calm again, and said 'Not what I want, but what you want, Father.' Then he knew that his journey to the cross was nearing its end.

## Part 2 – The cross

The journey to the cross was a long one, right up the bleak hill on the edge of Jerusalem. Jesus had been beaten and tortured, and he was tired as he dragged and carried the cross up the hill. He saw the faces of the crowd, some laughing and smiling, others crying and in despair. Jesus had known all along that the journey to Easter would end this way, but it was still hard and painful for him. He knew that he would have nails put into his hands and feet, and that he would not be able to breathe. This sad end was what his whole life had been for, but he also knew that there would be a new beginning.

The disciples had to watch as Jesus died so dramatically. The despair they must have felt is hard to imagine, and the confusion when they heard and saw evidence of the resurrection is impossible to describe. But there was a reason, a reason which changed history, and can change us. The new beginning was not just for him but for everyone who believes in him too.

## Eggstraordinary Easter

This is a popular approach to the Easter story, and can be done in a number of ways. You may want to split it over a number of weeks, or tell it as a complete narrative. The basic idea is that you tell the Easter story, using as many words as possible which sound as if they begin with 'eggs'. As you tell the story ask everyone to shout out the word 'eggs' or cluck like a hen whenever they hear you say 'eggs'. Have some mini-eggs available, and give one out to the loudest or the first person to shout or cluck each time. The words and phrases you may wish to use are listed below:

- The disciples had seen Jesus do eggstraordinary things.
- The disciples knew that Jesus was eggstra special.
- Jesus tried to eggsplain that he was going to die.
- As Jesus rode into Jerusalem they didn't eggspect a big crowd.
- The people were very eggsited, waving their cloaks and palm leaves.
- Jesus eggspressed his anger at how the temple was being used.
- The crowd eggsclaimed, 'Crucify him'.
- Judas decided that the people wanted to eggsecute Jesus.
- Jesus was eggstremely sad as he saw the people watch him being crucified.
- The nails were eggscruciatingly painful.
- Jesus finally eggspired, and the sky went black.
- The next morning there was eggstraordinary news.
- The disciples could not eggspress their joy!
- Jesus eggsplained to them that he really was alive again.

## Counting Easter

Before you begin, ask the congregation to immediately shout out any numbers that they hear you say. You may want to practise this before you give the following introduction.

Are there any adults here who enjoy doing their accounts? Are there any children who enjoy doing maths? I'm sure all of us have got confused with numbers sometimes, added two figures up wrongly, or found that we have run out of numbers.

Numbers can tell us a lot. We can add them up, subtract them, multiply them, or divide them. We can write them down as words or as figures. But most of all, numbers can tell stories!

Jesus was going to have to die. He had upset the powerful people and the rich people, and they plotted to kill him. In the end they decided to put him to death by nailing him to a cross of wood, using **four nails**. As Jesus walked up the hill to where he was set to die he saw that there were already **two robbers on crosses**. They had done wrong things, but Jesus hadn't. But Jesus had told his friends that **three days later** he would come alive again . . . but they hadn't understood. Jesus was put on the wood, and the **four nails** were hammered in. He was then left to hang, with the **two robbers on crosses** either side of him.

As Jesus hung there in the heat of the day a group of soldiers sat near him, and **one die was shaken**. They had all of Jesus' clothes, and were splitting them up between them. As the **one die was shaken** the soldier who guessed the correct number got the garment.

Jesus finally died, and hung there until, at **6 o'clock in the evening** a man came and took him to a large tomb. Not long after **6 o'clock in the evening** Jesus' dead body had been wrapped up and placed in the tomb, with a big stone and two guards outside it.

**Three days later** the most amazing thing happened. **Five people at the tomb** saw that the stone had been moved and that the body had gone. The **five people at the tomb** were two dazed and confused guards, two women who had been Jesus' friends, and one angel. The angel explained that Jesus was alive again – he was God, and could not be killed.

So despite that **one die was shaken** to split up Jesus' clothes, **two robbers on crosses** dying in the same way, **four nails** hammered in, the burial at **6 o'clock in the evening**, it took **five people at the tomb** to see that **three days later** Jesus really had come alive again, and live for ever!

## Would you believe it?

This story has a number of points where you should stop an invite the congregation to answer the question 'Would you believe it?' It would help if you have a radio mic and can go amongst the congregation to ask them their answers, making sure you choose a mixture of ages.

After all he had seen Jesus do and all the miracles he had witnessed, still the disciple Thomas didn't quite believe it! *Would you believe it?* He was always looking on with a puzzled frown on his face, always the one to ask Jesus to explain things again after he had already done so. *Would you believe it?* He was always the one walking a few metres behind the others.

'Thomas, are you listening?' Peter called to him one day as the disciples walked with Jesus through corn fields in Galilee, heading for Jerusalem and Jesus' last few days before being hung on the cross. 'Um, what was that?' mumbled Thomas. 'Listen,' said Peter, 'Jesus is explaining where he is going after his time on earth is over. This is important.' Thomas listened but he wasn't at all sure that it made sense. He had tried to learn to trust and not to doubt, but somehow he always wanted things clearer than they were. *Would you believe it?*

'Jesus, Jesus, can I ask a question?' shouted Thomas from the back of the group. Jesus stopped and turned round, a weary smile on his face. He was used to Thomas and his doubts, so he patiently said, 'Yes Thomas, ask away.'

'It's just that I don't understand where you are going, so I don't know how you will get there, and . . . and . . . well, I'm just not sure!' The disciples all sighed, and Jesus quietly explained that Thomas had to learn to trust, it was as simple as that! *Would you believe it?*

The next few weeks were very hard for Thomas and all the disciples. Jesus was a superhero as he healed people and rode into Jerusalem on a donkey, but soon became hated as he was arrested and accused of crimes he had never committed. *Would you believe it?*

The disciples were powerless to help as Jesus was nailed to the cross, and they cried in despair as he was put in a tomb. And all the time Thomas didn't quite trust that Jesus was in control. He thought that somehow Jesus had failed, and all that they had done had been a waste of time. *Would you believe it?*

Two days after Jesus died strange things began to happen, things which confused and excited all of Jesus' followers. Some of the women who had visited the tomb early that morning said that it was empty and that an angel had told them that Jesus was alive. *Would you believe it?*

When they told Thomas he thought they had gone mad! Jesus went to the room where some of the disciples, but not Thomas, were meeting and praying, and spoke to them. *Would you believe it?* When Thomas heard he thought they had all gone potty! 'Unless I actually see and touch those nail holes and the scar in his side I will never believe!' Thomas said. *Would you believe it?*

A week later they were all gathered again, Thomas sitting thinking at the back of the room. Quietly and quickly Jesus appeared in the middle of the room. As Thomas looked up he gasped. *Would you believe it?* 'Come, Thomas,' said Jesus, 'here are my wounds. Now you can see them, do you doubt, or do you trust?' Thomas was only able to stammer, 'My Lord, my God!' as he knelt at Jesus' feet and realised that he had never had any reason to doubt.

At Easter we have the same choice. We can think of all the things Jesus does, but still not believe that he came alive. Or we can believe the Bible and accept that Jesus did come alive again, and he did it for us. *Would you believe it?*

# I couldn't believe my eyes!

This talk is a monologue for a woman to read or learn, preferably wearing a simple costume. Ask the congregation to repeat *I couldn't believe my eyes* every time that phrase is used.

It was so sad. We had been with Jesus through the good times, and to see the crowd all calling for him to be put to death, well, *I couldn't believe my eyes!* The walk up the hillside was so sad, and then watching as those nails were put into his side, and seeing the pain in his face, *I couldn't believe my eyes!* We went with the body to the tomb and watched as Jesus was sealed up. *I couldn't believe my eyes!* And, well the cheek of it, we saw those guards placed next to the big stone. *I couldn't believe my eyes!*

The next couple of days were just dreadful. We didn't know what to do or what to think about, so we just went to the tomb a lot, and talked about the good times we had had with Jesus. But on that third morning, when we went to the tomb, well *I couldn't believe my eyes!* The stone had been moved out of the way and the body was not there. *I couldn't believe my eyes!* Then, to make matters even stranger, a bright shining light appeared, and two angels stood there, telling us that Jesus had come alive again. *I couldn't believe my eyes!* We looked on as the angels vanished, and *I couldn't believe my eyes!* We thought for a while that we had dreamed the whole thing, but the tomb was still open and empty. *I couldn't believe my eyes!* We rushed back to tell the other followers of Jesus, but they just stood looking miserable, and didn't believe us. *I couldn't believe my eyes!* But later, when more people said that they had seen Jesus, or heard that he was alive, we all started to hope. And finally we saw Jesus standing in our room among us. *I couldn't believe my eyes!*

After Jesus had been put on the cross we all thought that would be the end of it, but when I saw him alive again that day *I couldn't believe my eyes!* There he was, alive and real, eating food and talking to us. As I said, *I couldn't believe my eyes!* That was the beginning of a great few weeks when we listened to Jesus and tried to find out all we could. We knew he was special, now we were just beginning to realise just how special he was. Whatever he did, and whatever he said, *I couldn't believe my eyes!*

# Prayers

Lent is an important season to be quiet and listen to God, asking him to help us think through our own lives. Easter marks the culmination of Jesus' ministry, and a time of both sadness and celebration. Prayer is therefore of vital importance during both seasons. This selection of prayers include introductions, confessions, thanksgivings, intercessions and endings. They could be used on their own or supplemented by prayers from service books and *Common Worship*, or other prayers prepared by members of the congregation.

## Opening sentences

The spirit led Jesus into the wilderness.
(Matthew 4:1)

God's word says, 'Worship the Lord God and only serve him.'
(Luke 4:8)

All people will put their hope in him.
(Matthew 12:21)

And the power of the Holy Spirit was with Jesus.
(Luke 4:14)

Jesus will continue until he brings justice.
(Matthew 12:20)

Three days later he will be raised to life.
(Matthew 20:19)

God has kept his promises, and has come to save his people.
(Luke 1:54)

They will whip him and kill him, but after three days he will come alive again.
(Luke 18:32b-33)

God bless the King, coming in the name of the Lord.
(Luke 19:38)

May there be peace in heaven, and glory to God.
 (Luke 19:38)

My temple will be a place for prayer.
(Luke 19:46)

This is my body, which is given for you. Do this and remember me.
(Luke 22:19)

This man really was the Son of God!
(Mark 15:39)

I know you are looking for Jesus of Nazareth, who was crucified. He is not here, he has been raised to life!
(Mark 16:6)

Why look among the dead for someone who is alive?
(Luke 24:6)

Peace be with you always. As the Father sent me, so I send you.
(John 20:21)

# Prayers

**We are open to God,**
we are open to his leading.
**We are open to God,**
we are open to his speaking.
**We are open to God,**
we are open for his forgiveness.
**We are open to God.**

As we sit in quietness,
**we will get ready, get ready for God.**
As we put our thoughts aside,
**we will get ready, get ready for God.**
As we calm our hearts,
**we will get ready, get ready for God.**
As we think of worship,
**we will get ready, get ready for God.**

As we find space
show us your ideas,
**show us your ideas.**

As we think about our lives
show us our faults,
**show us our faults.**

As we give up all wrong
show us all that is right,
**show us all that is right.**

We think of Jesus, on his own in the wilderness,
**we thank you, Jesus.**
We think of Jesus, starving and tired,
**we thank you, Jesus.**
We think of Jesus, tempted and threatened,
**we thank you, Jesus.**
We think of Jesus, strong and determined,
**we thank you, Jesus.**

# Give-away to God

Hand out small pieces of paper and pens to all the congregation.

Ask them to think and write on one side something about themselves that they would like to give up. It may be a way of doing things, an attitude, or characteristic such as temper! On the other side they can write one practical thing that they could give up for Lent, such as chocolate, sweets or junk food. Younger children may need help with this.

Ask the congregation to pray silently, thinking about all that Jesus gave up in human terms (food, friendship, drink, sleep), and in spiritual terms (power, adoration, worldly worship). If appropriate, invite everyone to come to the front and place their pieces of paper in a frying pan as a sign of giving their sacrifices to God.

Jesus is coming to save his people,
**Jesus, please save me.**
Jesus is coming to lead his people,
**Jesus, please lead me.**
Jesus is coming to die for his people,
**Jesus, you died for me.**

Jesus, you rode into Jerusalem on a donkey,
**thank you that it isn't rumour, thank you that it is true.**
Jesus, the crowds cheered and called your name,
**thank you that it isn't rumour, thank you that it is true.**
Jesus, you spoke truth that people didn't want to hear,
**thank you that it isn't rumour, thank you that it is true.**
Jesus, you were hunted and arrested for doing no wrong,
**thank you that it isn't rumour, thank you that it is true.**

The Lord is risen,
**he is risen.**
The Lord is with us,
**he is risen.**
The Lord will always be here,
**he is risen.**
The Lord will always love us,
**he is risen.**

You knew it had to happen,
**you went to the cross for us.**
You carried your cross up that hill,
**you went to the cross for us.**
You had the nails hammered in,
**you went to the cross for us.**
You hung there in pain and shame,
**you went to the cross for us.**
You knew the end was coming,
**you went to the cross for us.**
You died, taking our wrong,
**you went to the cross for us.**

Let us think of the things of Easter.
Let us think of the eggs, the meals, the family.
Let us think of the good news, services and celebrations.
Let us think of Jesus, dying and living for us.

Let us share the news that Jesus is alive
in our homes and with our family.
Let us share the news that Jesus is alive
on our streets and in our community.
Let us share the news that Jesus is alive
in our work or at our school.
Let us share the news that Jesus is alive
in all we say, all we think, and all we do.

**We thank you, Jesus,**
you lived for us.
**We thank you, Jesus,**
you died for us.
**We thank you, Jesus,**
you live for us.

Jesus Christ is risen,
**yes, Jesus is risen.**
Jesus Christ is living,

**yes, Jesus is living.**
Hallelujah Jesus,
**yes, hallelujah Jesus!**

## Nails

Give each person in the congregation a blunt nail. You may want to file sharp ones down to ensure safety. Ask them to hold the nail in the palm of their hand while you lead them in the following:

The nail reminds us of pain. We think of the pain that Jesus felt.

The nail reminds us of the cross. We think of the robber's cross where Jesus died.

The nail reminds us of hands. We think of Jesus' hands, used to do good.

The nail reminds us of love. Jesus died to show us his love.

Good news, that Jesus died to save us,
**good news for us to share.**
Good news that death was just the beginning,
**good news for us to share.**
Good news that the grave could not keep him,
**good news for us to share.**
Good news that Jesus lives for everyone,
**good news for us to share.**

I celebrate that the stone was moved,
**my heart praises God.**
I celebrate that the grave was empty,
**my heart praises God.**
I celebrate that the angels waited,
**my heart praises God.**
I celebrate that the disciples believed,
**my heart praises God.**
I celebrate that Jesus rose again,
**my heart praises God.**
I celebrate that Jesus lives now,
**my heart praises God.**

# Intercessions

We pray for all people who do not know the good news that Jesus lives for them.

Jesus, **Jesus, be with us and hear us now.**

We pray for all people who have had bad, sad and upsetting news.

Jesus, **Jesus, be with us and hear us now.**

We pray for all people who are tempted to do wrong.

 Jesus, **Jesus, be with us and hear us now.**

We pray for places in the news where there is no peace today.

Jesus, **Jesus, be with us and hear us now.**

We pray for ourselves at this Easter time.

Jesus, **Jesus, be with us and hear us now.**

We pray that the cross will mean more than ever before.

Jesus, **Jesus, be with us and hear us now.**

We pray that you would give us new life now.

Jesus, **Jesus, be with us and hear us now.**


We pray for all those in your world, rich and poor,

**you died to give them life.**

We pray for our country and our leaders,

**you died to give them life.**

We pray for all believers in your Church,

**you died to give them life.**

We pray for all people in our community,

**you died to give them life.**

We pray for ourselves, that we would find you again this Easter,

**you died to give us life.**


We think of those who do not know the love of Jesus. We pray for those who are lonely, sad or ill. In particular we pray for . . .

We think of those who do not feel the love of Jesus. We pray for those who have no money, no home, or no family. In particular we pray for . . .

We think of those who do not understand Jesus. We pray for those who blame God for hard times, or have no one to celebrate Easter with. In particular we pray for . . .

We think of ourselves as we celebrate Jesus this Easter. We pray that we will all find time to make room for Jesus.

We pray for your world, that people who suffer would be helped.
**We pray to you, that your new life would bring life to others.**
We pray for our country, that it would look to you at this time.
**We pray to you, that your new life would bring life to others.**
We pray for our church, that we would share the good news.
**We pray to you, that your new life would bring life to others.**
We pray for ourselves, that we would welcome Jesus again.
**We pray to you, that your new life would bring life to others.**

## Responses for Intercessions

Lord, hear us as you live for us.

Lord Jesus, dying on the cross and rising from the tomb, please hear our prayer.

We bring these prayers to you, hear us this Easter we pray.

We pray to you this Lent.

Lord, in your mercy and through your love, hear our prayer.

As we open ourselves to you, help us we pray.

Please God, who gave your Son to die, hear us and help us.

As we are quiet please hear us, Lord.

Jesus, come to us and help us we pray.

At this special time please bring us new life.

# Endings

Jesus had the strength to resist temptation.
May that strength protect us also. Amen.

Help us always to be open to you.
**Help us as we go.**
Help us always to find time for you.
**Help us as we go.**
Help us always to look to the future with you.
**Help us as we go.**

So may the joy of the resurrection, the new life that Jesus shares, and
the power of the Holy Spirit be with us this Easter and evermore. Amen.

Jesus is risen,
**Let us share in his life. Amen.**

Let us go from here and prepare for new life in Jesus.
Let us go from here and prepare for new love in Jesus.

May the rising of Jesus encourage us.
May the rising of Jesus help us.
May the rising of Jesus change us. Amen.

May the blessing of the Father who sent his Son,
the Son who was willing to walk the path of death,
and the Holy Spirit who remains in us,
be with us all evermore. Amen.

Jesus came to the world to save us and change us.
Let us allow him to save us and change us.

As we prepare to remember the sacrifice of the cross
**send us out to explain that sacrifice.**
As we prepare for the good news of the resurrection
**send us out to share the good news.**
As we prepare in church and at home

**send us out to get our lives ready.**
As we prepare in our minds and hearts
**send us out to get our hearts ready.**

Be with us, Lord, as we go into this busy world.
Be with us, Lord, as we do all that has to be done.
Be with us, Lord, as we make time to meet you.

We are his people, he is our God
**Go with us now we pray.**

The Lord has risen to life.
**He has risen to life.**
Let us share his life.
**We will share his life.**

God's joy be in our hearts
this Easter and for evermore. Amen.

May the God who sent his Son to die for all people be with us.
May the Son who was willing to suffer on the cross be with us.
May the Spirit who brings life to our lives stay with us. Amen.

Let us go to share the good news.
Let us go to spread the good news.
Let us go to live the good news. Amen.

We remember the life and love of Jesus.
**Thank you, Jesus, for living for us.**
We remember the pain of death.
**Thank you, Jesus, for living for us.**
We remember the new life.
**Thank you, Jesus, for living for us.**